101
TIPS
for
MARRYING
the
RIGHT PERSON

"The most important part of marriage preparation begins long before the engagement. In *101 Tips for Marrying the Right Person*, Jennifer Roback Morse and Betsy Kerekes offer simple, straightforward, and sage advice on how to discern marriage with courage and conviction. If you want to build a lasting love, give your relationship a rock-solid foundation, and avoid the heartache of divorce, read these 101 tips!"

Jason Evert
Catholic speaker, author, and creator of The Chastity Project

"Finding a spouse is harder than ever in today's world. This book is full of succinct and practical tips to help navigate the challenging waters of dating. They address a wide variety of questions with answers that are insightful, relevant, and to the point."

Anastasia Northrop
Founder and director of the National Catholic Singles Conference

"Part reality check, part tip sheet, this page-turner will prepare your mind, heart, and soul for the most important decision you will ever make, and help you get it right the first time."

Tom Allen
Partner in Allied Faith and Family

"The dynamic duo of Kerekes and Morse have done it again. Engaged couples (and those seriously pondering marriage) finally have a discernment guide that is non-moralizing, non-churchy, and non-boring. The wisdom and good humor in this gem of a book should be required reading for Engaged Encounters and seminaries across the country. They hit all the right notes and ask all the right questions about the high adventure known as marriage."

Patrick Coffin
Catholic author, radio host, and podcaster

101
TIPS
for
MARRYING

the
RIGHT
PERSON

Helping Singles Find Each Other,
Contemplate Marriage, and Say I Do

JENNIFER ROBACK MORSE & BETSY KEREKES
of the Ruth Institute

AVE MARIA PRESS   AVE   Notre Dame, Indiana

Founded in 1865, Ave Maria Press is a ministry of the United States Province of Holy Cross.

www.avemariapress.com

Paperback: ISBN-13 978-1-59471-671-3

E-book: ISBN-13 978-1-59471-672-0

Cover design by David Scholtes.

Text design by Brian C. Conley.

Printed and bound in the United States of America.

Library of Congress Cataloging-in-Publication Data
Names: Morse, Jennifer Roback, 1953- author.
Title: 101 tips for marrying the right person : helping singles find each other, contemplate marriage, and say I do / Jennifer Roback Morse and Betsy Kerekes.
Other titles: One hundred one tips for marrying the right person | One hundred and one tips for marrying the right person
Description: Notre Dame, IN : Ave Maria Press, 2016. | Includes bibliographical references.
Identifiers: LCCN 2016026423 (print) | LCCN 2016034166 (ebook) | ISBN 1594716714 (pbk.) | ISBN 1594716722 ()
Subjects: LCSH: Marriage--Religious aspects--Catholic Church. | Mate selection--Religious aspects--Catholic Church. | Dating (Social customs)--Religious aspects--Catholic Church.
Classification: LCC BX2250 .M675 2016 (print) | LCC BX2250 (ebook) | DDC 241/.6765--dc23
LC record available at https://lccn.loc.gov/2016026423

Contents

A Special Note to Older People Buying This Book for a Young Friend

We're so glad that you're concerned about the prospects for love in your young friend's life. We wrote this book to help singles, especially young adults, navigate some of the common relationship pitfalls. But we have a secret for you and a favor to ask.

Basically, the young adult Catholic dating scene is horrific. Our most earnest young people are seriously trying to live their faith and be salt and light to the world, but they often find it difficult to meet other serious Catholics. Avoiding date rape drugs is a huge issue for many young adults. Finding someone who is committed to chastity can be an off-the-charts challenge.

To top it off, Catholic parishes don't usually have events geared toward young adult singles. They have programs for high school students, moms with preschoolers, and families with school-aged kids. Colleges have Newman Centers for college students. But few parishes have clubs or activities for young adults who aren't in college. Theology on Tap exists in some places, and is a great way for young working people to meet, but other than this, there isn't much out there.

So, here is the favor we ask of you: if you care about young people finding the right person to marry, try to do something to correct this.

Too much work, you say? For ordinary people, yes, maybe, but some of you have started bigger things than a monthly dance for twentysomethings. Some of you have homeschooled your children or started independent schools. Some of you have run businesses and capital campaigns. Some of you have put on massive charity events or modest parties. You have done all these things for your community and for your kids. Now do something for the young adult Catholics in your life. They'll thank you for it, and you'll be making a difference in their lives and in their chances of finding a good match. We thank you, too.

Your friends,
Jennifer and Betsy

INTRODUCTION

We all want reliable love in our lives. In this, we are no different than people in any other time in history, despite the tatters of failed marriages all around us. Holding this book in your hands proves that you're undaunted. You believe marriage can be, and is still meant to be, forever. This book will help you prepare for a lifetime of married love. You can use it by yourself or together, once you've found that special someone you think may be The One.

The One must be someone to whom you can be deeply committed. The first step is getting to a place where you're ready for marriage and are marriage material yourself. You'll want to take stock of any baggage or issues you may have and need to overcome. Next, this book will help you figure out what kinds of behaviors you think you can or want to overlook or put up with in another.

Our aim is to help you dodge the bullet, avoid trouble, and maximize your chances of success.

And success means having the opportunity to use all the tips from our first book, *101 Tips for a Happier Marriage*! That book inspired us to write this "prequel" because the very first step in having a happy marriage is to marry the right person in the first place.

Unfortunately, marriage discernment faces significant hurdles. Many people have already experienced so much relationship brokenness that they lack the conviction that real and lasting love is possible. Children of divorce don't want their children to experience what they went through themselves. Oftentimes children of divorce doubt their skills for keeping a marriage going.

To make things worse, we receive many confusing and conflicting signals from society around us. Our culture has dismantled many of the "guardrails" that used to keep people from making huge mistakes. Consequently, plenty of good, decent people are driving off the nearest cliff rather than forming lasting marriages.

We're here to help.

You can use this book from the time you start dating a potential spouse, right down to your wedding day. We begin in chapters 1 and 2 by helping you prepare yourself for marriage and search for the right person. You can read these chapters straight through, or you can read one tip per day to give you something constructive to think about and do.

We provide tips on dating and discernment in chapter 3. Once you've found a person you think may be right for you, chapter 4 offers you tips to reflect on privately or with a close friend. Chapters 5 and 6 give you and your potential spouse food for thought and discussion.

Most couples who present themselves for marriage preparation are already living together. Pastors and marriage prep teams struggle with how best to deal with this. If you're seriously involved with someone and thinking of moving in together, we offer considerations especially for you in chapter 7. And in chapter 8 we speak candidly to the reader who has already been cohabiting and who now wants to marry. Finally, chapters 9 and 10 offer more detailed reflection for you as a couple: questions to ask yourselves as you imagine your life together and questions to discuss as you reflect on your past.

There are two chapters on cohabitation because cohabitation is one of the most significant marriage preparation challenges faced by churches today. We don't tap-dance around it. We deal with it head-on. I (Jennifer) am sorry to say that not all my expertise in this area is "book learning." My husband and I cohabited before our marriage. I can attest that the research I report in this book is true.

The tips on cohabitation are designed to help you see for yourselves some of the issues that commonly arise when cohabiting couples finally get married. No matter what you may have thought when you moved in together, no matter who or what persuaded you that this was a harmless and beneficial thing to do, you have inadvertently taken on a set of risks for yourselves and your future marriage.

If you are cohabiting, we're not here to blame you or anyone else. We want to help you deal honestly with the situation in which you now find yourselves. If your pastor advises you to separate from each other as part of your marriage preparation, we wholeheartedly endorse this concept.

The Catholic Church has always taught that living in a sexual relationship outside of marriage is morally wrong, as do most other major religious traditions. Since we are both Roman Catholics and Ave Maria Press is a Catholic publisher, you won't be surprised to learn that we agree with this assessment. We want to share with you that the findings of modern studies on the negative effects of cohabitation are consistent with the Church's ancient teaching. We hope you can use this information to your benefit, no matter what your history may be.

The good news is that finding and being a worthy person to marry is indeed possible. Jennifer is a survivor of the sexual revolution and has patched together some right answers from doing many wrong things. Betsy is part of the younger generation of enthusiastic, faithful Catholics who have managed to navigate through the pitfalls of modern life by staying firmly on the Catholic path. Between us, we have a combined forty-five years of very different marriage experience. Let us help you pick a winner, while at the same time helping form you into the best, most marriage-ready version of yourself.

Your friends,
Jennifer and Betsy

THE SEARCH IS ON

Being Both Optimistic and Realistic

1

Expect some level of imperfection. Marrying a perfect person is impossible because no human is perfect.

However, there likely is a perfect someone *for* you: an equally imperfect fellow human being. Recognizing that you have flaws of your own will make this easier. Not only will you need to put up with someone else's imperfections, but he or she must put up with yours, too.

2

Make yourself worthy of the type of person you wish to marry. What do you need to work on before you're ready to get married? If you want to marry the right person, start planning now to *be* the right person.

What improvements can you make to be the person you want to be—the person who is ready for marriage, the person who will attract someone you want to spend the rest of your life with? If you need help dealing with past issues, disappointments, or baggage, you can consult a trusted friend, a spiritual adviser, or even a therapist. Become the best version of yourself for the sake of your own happiness and for your future marriage.

3

Know what you want in a potential spouse. Make a list of your needs versus wants. Don't cave on the needs, but be willing to budge on the wants.

Make those needs realistic. You don't *need* to marry an astronaut. A particular hair and eye color are not realistic needs either. Instead, think about the kind of personality that will challenge and bring out the best in you. What will help you find someone like this? For example, if you're intellectual and want your future spouse to complement you in this way, don't search for him or her at a dive bar. Or if you're athletic and want your spouse to also enjoy spending time at the gym or hiking outdoors, don't waste time dating a couch potato.

4

At the same time, be open to the unexpected. Allow God to surprise you in any way he wants. Sometimes people discover love when they're not looking for it. Take the pressure off yourself and just let God lead you unwittingly in the right direction.

I (Betsy) attended a wedding in which the best man shared in his toast that the groom had vowed never to marry a teacher; likewise, the bride had previously stated she would never marry a "computer nerd." And yet both had ended up doing exactly that! God has a sense of humor. Be OK with being blindsided by him. He knows what's best for you even better than you know yourself.

5

Relax. No matter how eager you are to get married, no matter how many disappointments you've experienced, panic is not your friend.

Try not to spend every waking moment thinking about getting married, pining for a spouse, dreaming about your wedding day, and naming your future children. Be patient and trust in the Lord. If it's meant to happen, it *will* happen, all in God's good time. Remember the old adage: let go and let God. If he intends for you to get married, your spouse is out there waiting for you.

6 _____

Pray.

Prayer is a way to keep you open and willing to follow God's plan for your life. Prayer also allows you to hear and feel his gentle nudging. Believe this: he wants you to be happy. Be encouraged and consoled when you're having a hard time being patient. Repeat this prayer from St. Faustina every time you feel anxious about finding the right person: "Jesus, I trust in you. Jesus, I trust in you. Jesus, I trust in you."

7

If you have no prayer life, get one.

Right away. For real. You think life is tough now, searching for the right person? Wait until you have to put up with each other—and kids. Seriously, get in the habit of prayer now. It provides peace of mind and comfort. The time you spend in prayer and meditation can bring you the insights you're looking for or even the insights you didn't know you were looking for. We urge you to seek divine help and not try going it alone.

8

Pray for your future spouse.

Pray that you find each other. Pray that the timing is right. Pray for his or her general happiness and well-being. You'll likely never know, in this life, the good that will come from praying for the person you'll eventually marry, but the positive effects will be there nontheless.

BEST PRACTICES

What to Do

9

Associate with people who share your values and interests.

If your faith is important to you, church activities and young adult groups are great options — singles' bars, not so much.

If your current group of friends shares your values and interests, they're a great start for finding a suitable marriage partner. If they don't, maybe you need a different group of friends.

10 _____

Be friends first.

Starting out as friends is an excellent, no-pressure way of getting to know each other without stress or expectations. If you discover down the line that you have feelings for each other, you can rest assured that it happened naturally. No one, yourself included, pressured you into it. You are dating for the right reasons.

We hasten to add: if you're already friends and are becoming interested in one another, don't be afraid to break out of the "just friends" mold. Guys, ask her out. Girls, you can let him know you're interested without coming off as pushy or aggressive. Invite him to go somewhere with you or to your house for a home-cooked meal. The point is to be brave. Don't stay in the "just friends" zone indefinitely if this person may be the one.

11

Go out with groups of friends.

A group date can reduce pressure, enabling you to relax and be yourself. After all, your real self is who you want the other person to see. Group dates also mean less temptation toward inappropriate behavior. When you're surrounded by other people, those opportunities don't present themselves.

12 _____

Ladies: let him be a man. Gentlemen: be a man!

Ladies, we realize this is retro, but allow yourself to be feminine. Allow him to be a gentleman. Be grateful when he opens the door for you. Let him treat you well.

Gentlemen, we know this is so twentieth century, but make the first move. Take the lead. She'll respect you for it. It's okay to woo her. Start now with the romance. She'll love you for it.

13

Remember that good looks are fleeting. Physical attraction is not enough to sustain a relationship.

If you're tempted by appearances only, you may have a problem in the marriage later on when your spouse's looks fade. It may sound cliché, but it's what's underneath the surface that truly counts and sustains a lasting relationship.

14 _____

Keep in mind that infatuation can mask itself as love.

If you can't get this person off your mind, that doesn't prove your relationship is real love. Puppy love can be a lot of fun, but it doesn't last. If you find yourself having intense feelings early in the relationship, try not to get carried away by them. Instead, step back and see how they stand the test of time.

15

Recognize that it is possible to fall in love with the wrong person.

It happens all the time. Sometimes engaged couples break up. Sometimes they break up the day before or the day of the wedding. Remember that an engagement is not a permanent covenant, but marriage is. Don't make the decision lightly.

16

When the relationship begins to get serious, seek the opinion of an objective third party, with emphasis on "objective."

Your best friend may be biased in your favor, too excited about the possibility of wedding planning, or simply afraid to tell you the truth. When you're so gaga in love, can you blame him or her, especially if it could mean ending your friendship? Find someone who knows you, loves you, and has nothing to lose by telling you the truth. Think parent or sibling. Resolve to listen to that person. Alternatively, ask yourself this: "If my best friend were dating this person, would I approve?"

17

Keep your head. Guard your heart.

Sometimes our imaginations carry us away into happily-ever-after prematurely. We may find ourselves forcing the relationship into the "perfect situation." We can rationalize that the other person lines up exactly with our plans. Instead, relax and let the relationship take its natural course. That way you can let it end when it should, if it should.

POTENTIAL PITFALLS

What Not *to Do*

18

Do not: Try to remake yourself or be defined by the person you're with.

If your personality is changing to better match that of this other person, he or she is probably not the right one for you. Take a break until you figure out who you are. Then you can figure out who you want to be with.

19

Do not: State all your faults on the first date in hopes of weeding out bad potential partners.

Why dump your baggage and scare the other person off before he or she gets a chance to know you? Let your inner crazy out little by little.

20

Do not: Expect a fairy-tale romance thanks to a childhood of Disney princesses and an adulthood of Jane Austen films.

This is real life. Your Prince (or Princess) Charming will not magically appear as you sing to the wildlife in the forest. (Nor will animals help you with your housework, unfortunately.) You're probably going to have to work to find him or her. Get used to the idea. This includes making yourself attractive and approachable.

21

Do not: Expect love at first sight.

Some people are sure they've experienced this, but there's no guarantee it will happen to you. Don't hold out for it, expecting your perfect soul mate to come find you or fall in your lap (or accidentally bump into you on the street). You'll likely have to work a little harder than that.

22

Ladies, *do not*: Dress like a floozy.

If you dress as if you have only your looks to offer, you'll attract shallow men who want and expect nothing more than a physical, short-lived relationship. Instead, dress to attract the type of man you'd want to marry. Good men are not interested in women with loose morals and, very likely, low self-esteem.

23

Gentlemen, *do not*: Be a slob.

Unless it is truly your dream to marry a fellow slob, put forth the effort to be attractive to her as well. Slovenliness for either or both of you is generally not a winning trait.

24 _____

Do not: Be with someone for the sake of not being alone.

This makes the relationship a selfish one from the start. Additionally, you'd be keeping yourself and the other person from being with whomever you're truly meant to be with. You'd only be setting yourselves up for a lot of hurt feelings and regret later on.

25 _____

Do not: Date someone you wouldn't consider marrying.

Sure, this person might be a lot of fun to be with, but why waste time on a meaningless relationship that you know is doomed to end in heartbreak for one or both of you? Be honest with yourself and with the other person. If you don't see this relationship going anywhere, why prolong the inevitable?

26

Do not: Date someone just to annoy your parents.

This should go without saying. You know this would be using someone. You wouldn't want someone to use you, so don't do it to someone else. It isn't fair to either of you. Figure out a better way to deal with your issues with your parents.

27 _____

Do not: Date someone to make the person you really want to be with jealous.

This, too, turns the person you're with into an object. It's unkind and immature. If the person you're interested in doesn't like you, try to get over it without manipulating or involving a third party. Then find someone else who does like you and whom you honestly like as well.

28

Do not: Waste time pining over someone who isn't into you.

You may find yourself fantasizing to the point of convincing yourself that you are meant to be together even though you're not even dating. In the meantime, the person who is right for you is waiting to be found. Move on so you can find him or her that much sooner. Accept that a romantic relationship with someone who just wants to be friends isn't meant to be.

29 _____

Do not: Look for "signs" from the Almighty that this person is the right one for you.

While you're at it, don't bother looking for images of the Virgin Mary in your toast. This is not the way God works. Don't read into anything as a sign from on high. If you're looking for that sort of thing, you might find it, but it will be of your own imagining.

30

Do not: Think you can change him or her into the perfect image of your future spouse. You can't.

Learn to live with whatever flaws you see, or find someone else who really is what you're looking for.

31

Do not: Waste your time on someone who won't commit to you.

If you've been dating for months but the other person still doesn't exclusively want to be with you, then stop and consider the time you're losing as you wait for him or her to make a decision. Is this person worth the wait?

32 _____

Do not: Think that just because you have invested so much time in a relationship it would be a shame to throw it away.

It would be a bigger shame to stay in the relationship just because you're already there. Cut your losses and move on.

33

Do not: Marry someone because you don't want to be alone or you don't think you'll have another opportunity.

Maybe you think this person is your best chance of getting married and having children. If you're meant to be married, the right person is out there waiting for you. Don't make a fear-based decision. If you walk down the aisle with the wrong person, you'll miss out on true happiness.

34 _____

Do not: Agree to marry someone because it's expected.

Just because your friends and family think you'll eventually tie the knot doesn't mean you have to. You shouldn't force something if it's just not right. We know people whose doomed relationships have gone even so far as engagement. The longer you put off the inevitable, the more difficult it will be to do what needs to be done. Take a hard look at your relationship. Despite what others may think and want, is staying with this person really the right thing to do?

35

Do not: Let past fears or concerns dictate whom you choose to be with now.

For example, a woman broke off a relationship with a man when she realized he was a porn addict. The next guy she dated was pure of heart, so she easily let herself believe he was the man for her despite other concerns. Though purity is most definitely an admirable trait that should be sought after in a potential spouse, this woman's judgment was clouded by the fear caused by her past relationship. They broke off the engagement shortly before the wedding. Make sure you marry someone for all the right reasons.

EARNEST QUESTIONS

Ask Yourself These before
You Get Too Serious

36

Can I picture myself spending the rest of my life with this person?

Anything less is a waste of time that could be spent with the person you *are* meant to be with forever. You're doing both of you a disservice otherwise.

37 _____

Can I see this person being the parent of my children?

Will he or she be someone who would raise them the way I'd want them to be raised? Can I picture this person as a good, solid parent and role model for my children? If not, move on.

38

Do I respect this person?

You need to be able to love this person uncondi-tionally until death do you part. If there's some-thing about him or her that you can't get over, then this person is not the right one for you. The sooner you accept and recognize that, the better.

39

Would I be proud to introduce this person to my friends and family?

If you find yourself making excuses for your potential spouse because you're ashamed of one aspect of his or her character or ability, that should cause you to reevaluate the relationship.

40

Do I feel at peace with this person?

This goes beyond a longing desire to be with someone, which is not a guaranteed indication of compatibility. When you're with this person, are you completely relaxed, with no nagging feelings of something being not quite right?

41

If you feel confident of your answers to the previous questions, ask yourself this to be sure: What is my reaction when I see this person for the first time after a long absence? Does my heart sing, or does part of it sink? Do I feel nothing at all?

If you're not ecstatic to see this person again, take a hard look at why that is. There may be an issue that you've been ignoring or justifying in your mind. Pay attention to those gut feelings.

42

Do I consider this person a fixer-upper?

It's wrong to picture yourself as the handyman (or handywoman) in charge of repairing the other person. If that term comes out of your mouth or pops into your mind, face it: you've got a problem. Figure out if you're the problem or if the other person really has serious issues you cannot live with.

43

Do I think of myself as settling for this person?

This term, as well as fixer-upper, is demeaning and unfair to him or her. Make a decision about what you can and cannot live with, and take responsibility for that. You aren't settling if you truly accept and love this person, faults and all. You're deciding to live with a perfectly imperfect person, which is, in the end, the only kind there is.

44

Does he or she show an interest in what is important to me?

For instance, does she come to an event with you even when she's tired? Does he show up and socialize even with that one friend of yours he finds annoying? A person who is truly in love with you and puts you first will go that extra mile, making personal sacrifices in order for you to be happy.

45

Does the other person care enough to help cheer me up when I'm down or commiserate with me when I'm upset—whichever I prefer?

Just as importantly, does he or she know and respect your preference, understanding that some people like the Pollyanna approach of looking on the bright side of a negative situation while some just want others to say, "That really stinks. I'm sorry that happened to you"? Figuring this out now, and respecting each other's wishes, even when they go against your natural inclinations, will be greatly appreciated in your future life together.

46

Are we respectful of each other's possessions?

Do you care enough about this person to treat what belongs to him or her without derision? Do you take good care of items borrowed? Do you both recognize that if something is important to the other person, it should be important to you as well? A person's possessions are a part of him or her. Take care of them as you would each other.

47

Is he or she a good listener? Am I?

Having great communication skills—both listening and speaking—will be crucial for lasting marital peace. If the two of you aren't great at verbally sharing with each other, listening and responding, work on improving those skills now. You'll definitely need them later on.

I (Jennifer) had a conversation with someone who had counseled hundreds of men over the course of his career. He said he'd never once met a man who left his wife for a better-looking woman. They left for women who listened more sympathetically. He may have been exaggerating, but this is definitely worth thinking about.

48

Do I frequently say nice things about him or her to my friends and family?

If you're so impressed with this person that you can't help gushing over how great he or she is, that's a good sign. Of course, don't put your friends off by being obnoxious about it. So you think you've got a keeper? Great. Trust us, they get it.

49

Do I ever find myself speaking unkindly behind the other person's back?

Bad-mouthing a person behind his or her back is not the behavior of a friend. If you're doing this, stop. Address your issue with the person face-to-face. Insist that the other person do the same. And if you occasionally have something negative to say, this doesn't necessarily mean he or she is wrong for you. But negative talk is something that, if carried into marriage, will be a strain on your relationship. Do your best to end the habit now.

50

How do the two of us handle disagreements? Do we accept that we're different people who think differently and are entitled to our own opinions?

Rolling with the punches (metaphorically speaking, of course) is a useful skill to cultivate in married life. Is this something the two of you attempt to do in your relationship now? Or do you fight frequently over small issues without achieving resolution? If minor skirmishes regularly lead to all-out war, you may want to call the whole thing off.

51

How is he or she at compromising? Does this person have to win every argument? Do I?

One of the most referenced sections in our first book, *101 Tips for a Happier Marriage*, is called "Recognize That Winning Is for Losers," where we observe that needing to win is not a sign of strength but a sign of weakness. Do you really want to spend the rest of your life with someone who needs to win all the time? Whether it's you or your intended, you might want to think this through.

52

Is he or she a huge flirt with others but says it's "harmless" or "meaningless"?

If it's bothering you, then it's not harmless or meaningless. Discuss this issue until either the problem stops or the relationship ends.

53 _____

Is he or she paranoid about my friendships with members of the opposite sex?

Honestly ask yourself if his or her concerns are valid and if you need to modify your behavior with others. Or perhaps your intended has insecurity issues that could evolve into unhealthy, controlling behavior. Regardless of the reason, get to the bottom of it and deal with it now.

54

Is he or she overly clingy?

This is a sign of internal issues, probably insecurities as well, that need to be worked out and overcome. If it makes you uncomfortable, you shouldn't have to deal with it.

55

Am I comfortable introducing my significant other to my family as they are? Or do I want to instruct my family on how to behave around this person?

If you're not secure enough letting your intended see your family as they really are, ask yourself why not. Is this an issue with your family or with your intended? Are you comfortable enough with this person to let him or her see your family's true colors? If you're secure enough to be yourself with this person, your family should be allowed to be themselves, too.

56

Ladies: How does he treat his mother? This gives you a clue as to how he is likely to treat you.

If he shows love, respect, and veneration for the woman who gave birth to him or the woman who raised him, you're in good shape. If he is disrespectful or dismissive, you've got a problem.

On the other hand, if his mother is running his life, that isn't a good thing either. If they're so cozy that there's no room for you, you've got a different kind of problem, but a problem nonetheless.

RED FLAGS

Aspects to Carefully Consider

Note: these risk factors aren't necessarily deal breakers, but they do require serious thought and candid discussion.

57

Is either of you a child of divorce?

Divorce is a traumatic event for children. According to Judith Wallerstein, who studied the impact of divorce on children for more than twenty-five years, the long-term effects of divorce crescendo in young adulthood as the person begins to seek relationships and intimacy for him- or herself. Trust issues, fear of rejection, and many other issues frequently emerge.

Don't be discouraged if either of you is a child of divorce. Instead, give this risk factor the seriousness it deserves. Get some help for whatever issues you may have. You'll improve your future married life if you begin your journey together with the honesty and vulnerability that this discussion will require.

58

Are you contemplating a religiously mixed marriage?

If so, you have a couple of options. The first is to plan now to live a lifetime this way. Both people believing their faith is absolute truth can cause understandable tension. You may have disunity in the family around worship practices and unshared expectations about handling significant life events. These issues may already be starting with your wedding.

Lack of shared expectations can create tension surrounding the timing and birth of children or how to raise them and may extend all the way to different expectations about funeral practices. If you're both devoted to your own faith and accepting of the other's beliefs, without trying to convert each other, you'll have a greater chance of success.

Your second option is to thoroughly hash out the significant differences between your faiths before marriage. In this case, go right ahead and try to convert each other, understanding that religious differences may become a deal breaker.

59 _____

Will your future spouse encourage or discourage your prayer life and your relationship with God?

If you're of different religions or different levels of faith, is your future spouse willing to go to church with you or at least allow you to raise your children in the faith? How will you handle questions such as, "Why do I have to go to church with Mommy? Why can't I stay home with Daddy?" or vice versa. Discuss this in advance and have a plan for dealing with it.

60

Has either of you been married before?

Second marriages are more apt to fail than first marriages. The problems that existed in previous marriages don't end with the marriage but are often carried into the next relationship. If you're the person with a past marriage, ask yourself what you've learned from that experience. What changes in your behavior and attitude will you bring to this marriage?

If your intended has had a previous marriage, do some serious soul searching. His or her version of events may be perfectly plausible and understandable, but you may still want to gather additional information. What do his or her parents, children, or siblings have to say about the first marriage and why it ended? Their interpretation can be revealing about your intended's character or about the character of your future in-laws. This can help you see whether this is really the right person for you. It can also prepare you for what's coming if you do marry this person.

We strongly urge you to follow the laws and procedures of the Church with respect to annulments before walking down the aisle. Presumably, your pastor will insist on this in any case.

61

Does either of you have children from a previous relationship?

If so, you have important questions to ask yourselves: How will your marriage affect the kids' lives? What are you prepared to do to ensure that these children feel fully part of the family if more children come along? Are you prepared for the possibility that they will not completely accept the new stepparent into their lives? Are you prepared to weed out any and all favoritism that so often arises when children are born into the new marriage?

Carefully consider the impact a family shake-up will have on your children. Will it still be worth it? Would you be willing to postpone this marriage until the children are older? Why or why not?

62 _____

Is either of you over age forty?

Keep in mind that older seekers are sometimes settled in their lifestyle. They may be less apt to comfortably and readily let someone else in, disrupting their routine. Maturity comes with age, but so can rigidity. Be honest with yourself about yourself and your intended.

63

Is either of you a user of pornography?

If neither of you uses pornography, that's great. However, please keep reading this tip. Surveys show that both men and women use pornography and that pornography is a major cause of divorce. More and more children are being exposed to porn at younger and younger ages. So you may have to deal with this at some point in your life together.

If you use porn, give it up now. If you won't give it up for the sake of your loved one and your marriage, you don't love him or her enough. If you can't give it up, you're addicted.

If your loved one uses porn, you have every right to ask him or her to stop. If you don't deal with the pornography issue now, when will you? When your six-year-old stumbles upon it on the computer? There will never be a better time to address this issue than right now.

If you both use porn, addiction is going to be an issue throughout your lives, whether you marry each other or not. We provide a few resources for you at the end of this book and on the Ruth Institute website. Good luck.

GREAT EXPECTATIONS

What to Discuss before Saying "I Do"

64

Have a candid conversation about what being open to life means to you.

What the Church means by "open to life" is that every act of sexual intercourse must be open to the possibility of conception, no contraception involved. You're not obligated to have sex all the time, so you can use fertility awareness methods as a means of spacing pregnancies if you have serious reason to do so, which we'll discuss more in the next tip. Do you intend to plan your pregnancies right down to the minute? (I, Jennifer, tried that. I don't advise it. It may sound good on the drawing board, but God has a way of laughing at our plans.) Or are you a "come what may" kind of person? Discuss this thoroughly.

For the record, a study from Ohio State University has shown that adults from families with three or more children have lower divorce rates. Researchers speculate that this is because children from large families are better at relating to others, learning to share, not being selfish, doing without, and dealing with lots of personalities. The benefits taper off after seven children.

65 _____

Discuss how each of you feels about Natural Family Planning.

Natural Family Planning, also referred to as NFP, is morally acceptable when you have a serious reason to use it. These two Church documents should give you plenty to talk about:

According to paragraph 16 of *Humanae Vitae*, a papal encyclical by Pope Paul VI, a married couple may morally space births for serious reasons "arising from the physical or psychological condition of husband or wife, or from external circumstances."

The Vatican II document *Gaudium et Spes* states in paragraph 50, "Let them thoughtfully take into account both their own welfare and that of their children, those already born and those which the future may bring. For this accounting they need to reckon with both the material and the spiritual conditions of the times as well as of their state in life."

We strongly recommend that you sign up for an NFP class, no matter what your religious convictions may be. You'll learn a great deal about the natural cycle of a woman's body as well as communication skills that will help you in your married life. You'll also likely meet a group of nice people who will be eager to support you.

66 _____

Consider how you'll feel if you discover you can't have children. Have a plan of action ready in case God throws you that curveball.

What can you picture yourself doing or not doing if you can't have as many children as you want? Will a fertility crisis break you? Can you agree on how to handle it? NaPro Technology applies the principles of Natural Family Planning to the problem of trying to conceive. This method has excellent results for overcoming infertility problems while staying in line with Catholic teaching.

Will you consider adoption? What other outlets can you think of for the maternal and paternal parts of your personality?

67

Discuss how you'd educate your children.

This doesn't need to be a heavy, hand-wringing drama. It can be a fun discussion that leads to learning more about your significant other's childhood.

Will your future children go to Catholic school, public school or be homeschooled? Will you let them grow up watching anything they want on TV? Differences of opinion in these matters are good to work through even in the early stages of a relationship.

68

Take a close look at each of your approaches toward money: saving, spending, and giving.

Do you have a similar mind-set on how you'll handle your finances? Will you budget? Will you tithe? Is one of you thrifty and the other a spendthrift? Finances are among the top causes of marital discord, so decide on a plan of action now.

Here are some basics you should try to see eye to eye on:

- Debt (An antidebt absolutist is not going to do well with a we-can-save-money-in-the-long-run-by-borrowing-today kind of person.)

- Impulse spending (A person who spends to calm anxieties may have a hard time with someone who can't even relate to the concept.)

- What you each count as "security" (Do high-risk investments make you crazy? Does the thought of two weeks without a job scare you?)

- Giving (Is tithing of your money, time, or talent equally important to both of you?)

69

Are you coming from different financial backgrounds?

This, too, can cause stress. Is there underlying tension as a result that needs to be resolved now? Discuss this and work it out. Also, your financial and social background can heavily influence big decisions down the line (think wedding extravagance, the type of car you drive, and so forth). It's a good idea to begin thinking about how the two of you might differ on these issues and where you agree.

70 _____

Evaluate your significant other's relationship with his or her parents as well as your relationship with your own parents. Do this both separately and together.

Here are some factors to consider when dealing with in-laws. These aren't deal breakers, but they're worth observing and discussing.

- Does your intended have unresolved issues with his or her family? For most people, the answer will be yes. Can you see yourself hanging in there with your intended while he or she works through those issues? Can you live with someone with those issues?

- Do you consider your future in-laws charmingly weird or truly crazy? What, if anything, do their quirks tell you about your intended and what he or she might be like to live with?

After considering these issues for your intended's family, consider them for your own. What baggage do you bring that you can begin dealing with now, before marriage? And what strengths do you bring from your family that you can begin building on?

71

Observe how your future in-laws behave around your intended and their other grown children, if they have any. Family get-togethers for holidays and special events, as well as ordinary family interactions, can give you clues about what level of involvement to expect from them.

You may differ over what's considered normal family involvement. These differences can bring about fruitful conversations for the two of you. What does each of you expect to happen when your children are born? Will your mother-in-law want to stay with you for a month afterward? If so, are you okay with that? And if not, will your spouse side with you over his or her mother? Differences in these matters are worth discussing, as in-law involvement can be a cause of marital strife.

72 _____

Discuss the family and holiday traditions that meant a lot to you as a child and which ones you'd like to see continued in your future family.

Everyone's family has different ways of celebrating. What traditions are negotiable for you and for your intended? Discuss how you'll incorporate your different family traditions fairly and amicably. Can you anticipate any tension regarding where to spend holidays? See if you can resolve those issues in advance.

73 _____

Consider each of your expectations for the wedding day.

Discuss your views on keeping it simple versus being extravagant. How do you each define a small wedding? Or if one of you wants a big wedding, what exactly do you mean by that? Don't leave room for stressful surprises!

74

Beware of prenuptial agreements.

If you or your intended has created a back door
for the relationship, chances are one of you will use
it. If you feel a prenuptial agreement is necessary,
then you aren't right for each other, and a part of
you, whether consciously or unconsciously, realizes
that.

COHABITING

Should You?

75

Consider this if you're thinking about moving in together: the National Marriage Project did a thorough review of all the research on cohabitation. They concluded that "no positive contribution of cohabitation to marriage has ever been found."

Many couples move in together believing it will help them have a happier marriage. If you're one of those couples, the National Marriage Project results should be a wake-up call. Why get involved with something that, despite what you may otherwise hear, has nothing positive to contribute to your future marriage?

76

Be aware that sex makes us physiologically attached to our partners. You may think that sleeping together will help you discern whether or not you're compatible, when in fact it serves to cloud your judgment.

Sexual activity releases oxytocin, sometimes called the "attachment hormone." It creates feelings of relaxation and bonding, especially for women. Men attach through a hormone called vasopressin, sometimes called the "monogamy hormone." In either case, our bodies go on autopilot, connecting to our sex partners. We think our judgment is rational, but often our minds are clouded by the flood of hormones. This involuntary chemical commitment counterbalances the benefits we think we're receiving from getting to know each other while living together.

77 _____

Remember that breaking up is hard to do, whether you're cohabiting or married.

Sometimes couples think living together will protect them from the pain of a separation. This isn't true for two reasons. First, cohabiting relationships are actually more likely to break up than marriages. Only 40 percent of couples have gotten married after three years of cohabiting. And secondly, don't kid yourself: the breakup of a cohabiting relationship can be painful and complicated. Maybe it's not quite as bad as a divorce, but it's no picnic just the same.

78 _____

Ignore the hype from popular culture: couples who live together prior to marriage are *more* likely to divorce than those who don't.

Television sitcoms and movies are not scientific studies. If you view a lot of pop culture, you may be getting a steady diet of the message that living together is no big deal. These programs typically don't show you the couples who live together, get married, and get divorced, which is what studies suggest frequently happens. And movies and television surely do not show you the misery of people who live together and regret wasting big chunks of their life with someone who won't make a commitment. Who are you going to believe: Hollywood or scientific studies?

79

Before you move in, ask yourself this: What if we end up not getting married? How would you feel if this relationship broke up and you had to start over with someone new?

Some researchers claim that only serial cohabiting is associated with a higher divorce risk. That is, if you marry the person you're living with and that is your only cohabitation experience, your chances of divorce are no higher than anyone else's. But that research overlooks a very important point: you don't know for sure whether you'll ultimately marry this person when you move in with him or her. If you break up, you now have an episode of cohabitation under your belt. You've inadvertently set yourself up to become a serial cohabiter, which actually does have a higher risk of divorce.

80

Look around at people you know who have cohabited or are cohabiting with this question in mind: Does the cohabiting experience mean the same thing to each of them?

You don't need to ask pointed questions to come to a reasonable conclusion that cohabitation often means different things to different people. You may discern it from the jokes they tell, from the topics they avoid, or from the language they use to describe their relationship. Are they respectful toward each other? Is there an edge to their teasing and jokes? Do they denigrate the relationship or the other person?

It isn't unusual for the woman to think that moving in together is a step toward marriage while the man thinks living together is a perfectly acceptable long-term situation. But regardless of their different interpretations, your observations may tell you this: these cohabiting relationships often have a mismatch from the beginning. When problems arise, the woman may have a tendency to not rock the boat and brush the problems aside. The man may not wish to be pressured to make a commitment. Both of these tendencies can cause the couple to avoid addressing issues that should be addressed. These issues would be more easily addressed without living together and without the daily question mark hanging over their relationship: Are we going to get married or not?

81

Ignore those who claim that marriage is an old-fashioned, out-of-date institution that's harmful to people, especially women, and who hint that cohabiting is better for all concerned.

A permanent commitment between their parents is best for children. So if you plan to have children, there is nothing old-fashioned or out of date about marriage. I (Jennifer) have noticed that many sociology professors make the claim that marriage is awful, but they seldom answer the question, Compared to what? If they did compare marriage to the most likely alternative, cohabitation, they'd find that marriage is better than living together for all concerned.

82 _____

Be aware that a long-term cohabiting situation often puts women at a disadvantage compared to men.

The older the man gets, the more women are available for dating and eventual marriage. By contrast, the woman's fertility and her chance of finding a husband decline with each passing year. He has more alternatives than she does, on average. This mismatch may make the woman more likely to strain to keep the relationship going while the man is less concerned with permanence. You may think this is unfair; nevertheless, there is too much truth in it to ignore.

83

If you're scientifically minded, take note: the problems we have discussed so far really are due to cohabitation itself. This issue has been thoroughly studied. It's *not* just that the kind of person who cohabits would be more likely to have problems in the first place, whether he or she cohabited or not.

I (Jennifer) have given lots of talks on this subject, and I frequently hear this: "The people who are most likely to cohabit are poor, uneducated, and otherwise lower-class people who are more likely to have problems anyway. Since I am a well-educated, higher-income, and all around nicer person, it won't happen to me. Cohabitation looks like a bad deal because people who cohabit tend to be losers in the first place."

So, are you volunteering to join the ranks of the "losers"? Besides, the idea that cohabiters are systematically different, and that this can account for their poorer outcomes, turns out not to be true. Researchers have held constant all kinds of variables, such as age, education, and income. They've even looked at whether people who cohabit today have fewer problems than people who cohabited years ago when it was more heavily stigmatized. Regardless of these differences, the results show a higher probability of divorce and relationship instability for couples who have cohabited.

84

Ask yourself this question: With all the risks associated with living together, do you really think you can beat those odds?

If so, why do you believe this is the case? Don't deceive yourself. What makes you think you're different and more special than everyone else?

85

If either of you has children and you're considering moving in together, don't.

Living with a mother's cohabiting boyfriend is statistically the most dangerous living arrangement for children. In one study, such children were fifty times more likely to be killed from inflicted injuries than children living with their biological parents married to each other.

If your intended is a good guy and would never do a thing like that, great. Marry him. Don't move in together. If you move in together, your children may grow to love him and become attached to him. In that case, a breakup will be very painful for your children. Why take the chance of putting your children through that?

If you aren't sure enough to marry, you aren't sure enough to move in. Solve your financial problems and loneliness some other way.

COHABITING

Are You?

86

Reflect on the level of trust you currently have in your partner and in your relationship. Ask yourself if you're satisfied at this level. If you're not satisified, you and your intended should make a plan for improving this. If you're not satisfied but your intended is OK with the trust level where it is, you may want to rethink your marriage plans.

Whether you intended to or not, you may have been rehearsing not trusting. Half a commitment is no commitment. Cohabiting couples have one foot out the door throughout the relationship. If this describes you, these behaviors of not trusting or of looking at the open door can come back to haunt you during your married life. Lack of trust is a big deal in married life.

87 _____

Pay attention to this issue: Have you been practicing using each other? If so, is this what you want your relationship to be?

While any relationship can become utilitarian for the sake of guaranteed companionship, cheaper rent, or easy sex, cohabiting is especially prone to this tendency. Cohabiting amounts to this: "I'm willing to let you use me as a commodity, as long as you allow me to treat you as a commodity." This, too, can come back to haunt your married life.

If this describes your relationship, here is a plan for dealing with it: Be generous toward him or her. Be grateful for what your partner does for you. Don't take him or her for granted. Generosity and gratitude are great antidotes for the mutual using of each other.

88

Be aware that the cohabitation experience seems to change people's behaviors and attitudes. If you later marry, you and your intended may have some issues to work on that carry over from the cohabiting phase of your relationship. Resolve to work on these.

For instance, research shows that cohabiting couples tend not to be as committed to continuing the relationship as married couples are. Cohabiting couples are typically more oriented toward personal autonomy. They often have fewer problem-solving skills and exhibit less supportive behavior when they do marry. Because long-term commitment is less certain in cohabitation, the National Marriage Project concludes, "there may be less motivation for cohabiting partners to develop their conflict resolution and support skills."

If you encounter any of these issues, understand that they may not be your fault. You moved in together not fully aware of these pitfalls. Resolve to be generous with one another as you work on these problems together.

89

If you have a history of infidelity in your relationship, ask for forgiveness, offer forgiveness, and make amends to each other, as needed.

Cohabiters, both men and women, are less likely to be faithful. If this applies to you, you obviously have something to work on. Infidelity may be a deal breaker if either of you is a sex addict.

However, honestly, did anyone ever tell you that cohabiting couples are more likely to be unfaithful? Or how much being cheated on hurts, even if you aren't married? If you had known this before you moved in together, would you have done it in the first place?

This is a problem that many couples face. There is so much confusion about sex and marriage that even decent, intelligent people do hurtful, stupid things. If you discovered that infidelity hurts more than you were led to believe, try to be gentle with each other.

90

Consider how your financial arrangements currently work. Ask yourself if you'd be satisfied with what you have as a long-term situation.

On average, cohabiting men work fewer hours than married men. They typically spend more time for themselves than for the relationship or family. They also have a higher unemployment rate. Not surprisingly, poverty is more common among cohabiting women and their children.

If you think this situation applies to your relationship, you have some serious thinking to do. If you're not happy with this, are you sure you're right for each other?

Ladies, if you think he should be contributing more, financially or otherwise, consider asking him to move out. If he balks, he isn't likely to change his behavior. We don't recommend getting married as a way of inducing him to work harder or behave more responsibly. If he's willing to move out and pull himself together financially, you may have a winner.

91

Give serious thought to the issue of domestic violence. If there's any hint of violence in your relationship, toward you or your children, get out now. If you're a perpetrator of domestic violence, take steps to change your behavior now.

Cohabiting couples have higher rates of domestic violence than married couples, as well as higher rates of both physical violence and sexual violence against children in the home. This fact isn't generally discussed in mainstream news outlets, or even academic or policy settings, but you're entitled to know.

92

One final tip for you: If you're cohabiting and considering marriage, move out. If moving out is not practical, move into separate bedrooms and live chastely until your wedding.

Living chastely allows you to focus on the other aspects of your relationship and see one another in a different light. It will give you a chance to test yourselves and your commitment to each other. Over the course of your married life, there may be times when you cannot be sexual with each other due to illness, work-related separation, or any number of things. Can you love one another without being sexual? This is an important test.

Besides, sex outside of marriage is morally wrong. You'll be preparing yourself for marriage by cleaning your spiritual house, so to speak. We know of priests who recommend this for their cohabiting engaged couples, including some priests who insist upon it. And we know of couples who have been truly blessed by it.

Trust us on this.

PERFECT TIMING

If This Is the One, Is Now the Time?

93

Make sure you're both mature enough for marriage. Neuroscience, via brain scans, has proven that most human brains don't reach full maturity until age twenty-five.

Age is not a dealbreaker, just a consideration. This merely suggests that if you're in your late teens or early twenties, you shouldn't be in a rush. That said, we know many couples, Betsy included, who married in their early twenties and maintained successful, happy marriages.

94

Take note of your financial situation, but don't stress over financial perfection.

Being in college or in debt might cause you to tap the breaks on your marriage plans. Or you may consider whether you could live with your parents or other more established adults. Would you find that embarrassing or a relief?

We don't recommend waiting until you have all your financial ducks in a row. That can become an excuse for dithering. It is quite possible to wait too long. Among the risks of waiting too long are becoming too materialistic or individualistic or being unable to have children. There is something to be said for working out your financial problems together, as a team.

95

Take the marriage preparation seriously.

I (Betsy) saw one couple cheating on the compatibility test by copying each other's answers. You aren't doing yourself any favors by not listening and taking to heart what the instructors have to tell you based on their knowledge and experience. The marriage preparation classes are a great time to discover any issues that need to be addressed.

96

Make sure there are no impediments to marriage.

Regardless of your religion, you may be interested to know how the Catholic Church defines impediments to marriage. Besides being too young, too closely related, or already having a valid marriage, the Church includes these items as issues that could invalidate a marriage:

- Coercion
- Psychological immaturity or mental incapacity
- Refusal to have children
- Exclusion of fidelity
- Permanent physical inability to consummate the marriage

The Church insists that both parties be fully prepared to perform the duties of marriage and that they make this decision freely. This is a good idea, regardless of your faith.

MARRIAGE PLANNING

Focus on the Marriage, Not the Wedding

97

Remember: This one day should be memorable, but it isn't as important as the rest of your lives.

Becoming Bridezilla and needing to get your own way is nothing to be proud of. You want to remember this day for its love, beauty, and celebration with family and friends, not for quarrels and anxiety. Take a deep breath, relax, and go with the flow. This one day, though extremely important, is not as important as the rest of your lives. Keep that in perspective.

98 _____

Now is a good time to learn to work together.

Yes, you may both have dreams and imaginings about what this day will be like, and those plans or ideas may not match up perfectly. Defer to one another whenever possible, especially by giving in to whomever feels most strongly about the particular matter at hand.

99

Now is a good time to begin budgeting together, even if one or both sets of parents are paying for parts of the wedding.

Pretend everything is your responsibility. If you were paying, would you want that super-sized floral arrangement or that sit-down dinner? Get some clarity between the two of you. Once you're clear on what is really important to you, discuss it respectfully with your parents. Be prepared to defer to others on small things (and you'll be amazed at how many things really are small). And, by all means, be grateful to your parents, your bridesmaids, your groomsmen, and anyone else who contributes to your special day in any way. Don't forget to thank them lavishly. It may be your day, but that doesn't mean they're not important and excited, too.

100

Now is a good time to begin putting each other first, ahead of your parents, friends, and families.

Of course you want to show due respect to your parents. One or both sets may have strong opinions about the wedding, especially if they're paying for it. But you need to start deferring to each other, not necessarily to your parents. You need to back one another up in disputes with others about significant issues.

101

Ask yourself one last time: Do I feel at peace with my decision to marry this person?

Is there anything gnawing at you that you keep shoving down, ignoring, or rationalizing away? You need to pull whatever that is up again and take a good look at it. Could your gut be telling you to break this relationship off? This is the rest of your life you're talking about. It's a more important decision than buying a car or house or choosing a career. All those things can be changed. Your spouse, on the other hand, cannot. Therefore, this is the biggest decision you'll make in your life. Do not make it lightly.

If you've made it this far, enjoy your lives together! We offer you our best wishes for lifelong married love!

REFERENCES AND ADDITIONAL READING

GENERAL

The Ruth Institute website (http://www.ruthinstitute.org) has resources for people who have been harmed by family breakdown, sexual permissiveness, and related problems. Pages especially relevant to those considering marriage include the following:

- Children of Divorce
- Children of Single Parents
- Reluctantly Divorced
- Cohabitors with Regrets
- Pornography Addicts and Their Families
- Refugees from the Hookup Culture
- Persons with Health Problems Due to Hookups, Contraception, or Abortion

Crenshaw, Theresa L. *The Alchemy of Love and Lust*. New York: Simon and Schuster, Pocket Books, 1997, 90–105.

"Marriage: Love and Life in the Divine Plan." Pastoral letter. United States Conference of Catholic Bishops. Washington, DC: 2009. http://www.usccb.org/upload/marriage-love-life-divine-plan-2009.pdf.

COHABITATION

"Should We Live Together? What Young Adults Need to Know About Cohabitation before Marriage: A Comprehensive Review of Recent Research." Rutgers, NJ: National Marriage Project, 2002. http://www.national-marriageproject.org/wp-content/uploads/2013/01/ShouldWeLiveTogether.pdf. The quotation in Tip #88 can be found on page 5 of this document, last accessed April 18, 2016.

Stanley, Scott M., and Howard J. Markman. "Working with Cohabitation in Relationship Education and Therapy." *Journal of Couple and Relationship Therapy* 8, no. 2 (April 2009): 95–112. http://www.ncbi.nlm.nih.gov/pmc/articles/PMC2897720.

DIVORCE

Wallerstein, Judith S., Julia M. Lewis, and Sandra Blakeslee. *The Unexpected Legacy of Divorce: The 25 Year Landmark Study*. New York: Hyperion, 2001.

Canonical Impediments to Marriage

A complete discussion of annulments and canonical impediments to marriage is well beyond the scope of this book, which has the limited objective of helping people choose the right spouse. We offer the following as background information.

Boudinhon, A. "Canonical Impediments." In *The Catholic Encyclopedia*. New York: Robert Appleton Company. Retrieved April 18, 2016 from New Advent: http://www.newadvent.org/cathen/07695a.htm.

For people who have been married and who believe their marriage may have been invalid.

Sweet Rose, *The Catholic Divorce Survival Guide*. Milwaukee: Ascension Press, 2010. http://www.catholicsdivorce.com.

For people who have been married and who believe their marriage was and therefore still is valid, and who wish to defend the validity of their marriage. Mary's Advocates. http://www.marysadvocates.org. Accessed April 18, 2016.

Pornography

Fight the New Drug. http://www.fightthenewdrug.org. Last accessed April 18, 2016.

Layden, Mary Anne, and Mary Eberstadt, eds. *The Social Costs of Pornography: Statement of Findings and Recommendations*. Princeton NJ: Witherspoon Institute, 2010.

If you're curious about the Ohio State University study mentioned in Tip #64, it is found here:

King, Nicole M. , "More siblings means less divorce risk." *MercatorNet*, August 17, 2013. http://www.mercatornet.com/family_edge/view/12630, Accessed April 18, 2016.

Jennifer Roback Morse, a renowned marriage and family scholar, is the founder and president of the Ruth Institute. She is the author of three books and the coauthor of *101 Tips for a Happier Marriage*. Her numerous academic and public-policy articles have appeared in such publications as the *Journal of Economic History, Forbes, Harvard Journal of Law and Public Policy*, and *National Review* online. She has spoken around the globe on marriage, family, and human sexuality, and her work has been translated into several languages. Morse earned her doctorate at the University of Rochester and taught economics at Yale and George Mason Universities. She and her husband live in Louisiana, and they have two grown children.

Betsy Kerekes is the coauthor of *101 Tips for a Happier Marriage*. Her professional experience includes working in journalism and public relations for Franciscan University of Steubenville, where she graduated summa cum laude in writing, with a minor in communications. She also did proofreading and subscriptions management for Patrick Madrid's *Envoy* magazine and has contributed to *Aleteia, MercatorNet, Catholic Lane, Catholic Exchange, CatholicMom. com, The Southern Cross*, and *Creative Minority Report*. Kerekes is a blogger and also serves as editor and director of online publications at the Ruth Institute, where she also writes weekly newsletters and manages the blog. She telecommutes from her home near San Diego, where she homeschools her three children.